Swimming
in Action

Duncan Goodhew

G000070011

Stanley Paul
London Sydney Auckland Johannesburg

Stanley Paul and Co. Ltd

An imprint of Century Hutchinson Ltd

Brookmount House, 62-65 Chandos Place
Covent Garden, London WC2N 4NW

Century Hutchinson Australia (Pty) Ltd
88-91 Albion Street, Surrey Hills, NSW 2010

Century Hutchinson New Zealand Limited
191 Archers Road, PO Box 40-086
Glenfield, Auckland 10

Century Hutchinson South Africa (Pty) Ltd
PO Box 337, Bergvlei 2012, South Africa

First Published 1988

Typeset in Monophoto Times by
Vision Typesetting, Manchester

Printed and bound in Great Britain by
Butler & Tanner Limited, Frome and London

British Library Cataloguing in Publication Data
Goodhew, Duncan
  Swimming in action.
  1. Swimming
  I. Title
797.2'1   GV837

ISBN 0 09 166441 1

Acknowledgements

All the photographs in this book were
specially taken by Roy Pell and Alec
Daniels.

Contents

Introduction

Most people suffer from impatience and want to become instant experts – but as the saying goes, Rome was not built in a day. You must first find out exactly what is involved in what you are trying to do. However, this can pose difficulties when learning to swim. The movements required are quick and difficult to see; and added to this, the most important motions of the stroke are obscured from vision beneath the surface of the water. This flicker book will give you a precise picture of the movements you want to achieve. It is not, however, a step-by-step 'learn to swim' manual.

Because water is a milieu with which most of us are unfamiliar, it is obviously worthwhile spending a few minutes concentrating on the fundamentals. Let's face it, becoming frustrated at not perfecting yourself is one thing; becoming terrified of drowning is another. So, first things first – here are the answers to some basic questions about swimming.

Learning

Sequence A:
Freestyle

Sequence B:
Backstroke

Sequence C:
Breaststroke

Sequence D:
Butterfly

When to learn to swim

Although there is no age restriction on learning how to swim, the earlier one starts the easier it tends to be. A personal recommendation is at about three to four months old (immediately after first immunisation). A baby of this age has little or no fear of the water, and generally learns quickly to enjoy it. If this is not a good enough reason then consider the pleasure parents get when their child learns to swim before it can take its first steps! But before you rush to the pool with your young baby, please read the sections that follow.

If you are not three or four months old, do not despair – it is never too late to learn.

Learning considerations

Never believe in the principle, 'sink or swim'. In other words, do not throw a non-swimmer into the deep end. It is completely inconceivable to me that anyone could inflict this kind of torture on another person. Just because *you* can swim does not mean someone who can't will not drown, or more to the point, believe himself to be drowning, and this belief can become real to a non-

5

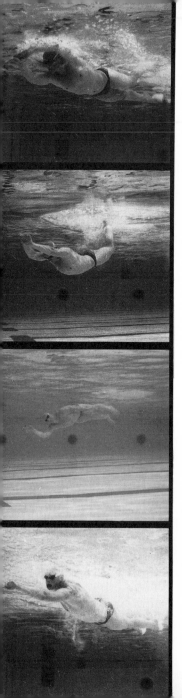

swimmer. If a non-swimmer is subjected to this kind of thoughtless behaviour, then there is a good chance that he will never get over his fear of the water.

How to learn to swim

The best way to learn to swim is to join a club. Most clubs have a 'learn to swim' programme, as well as regular coaching and training sessions which are for the competitive swimmers. After learning, if you are keen or show talent for swimming, you can continue the programme. Alternatively, Amateur Swimming Association (ASA) qualified instructors will coax you into becoming a proficient swimmer at your own pace. For further details contact your local swimming baths or write to the ASA, Harold Fern House, Derby Square, Loughborough.

Health

Polio vaccination

Although people think of polio as a disease of the past, it is not. It still exists, and there is concern that if people do not keep their vaccinations up to date there could be a serious resurgence of it. Polio is a particularly ugly disease which can be completely prevented by taking three drops of vaccination on a sugar lump every five years. You should not really swim without taking this precaution. Seek advice from your family doctor and check up on tetanus immunisation as well.

Ears

If you swim regularly, swimmer's ear can be a hazard. It is caused by skin in the ear becoming wet and irritated due to infection. Although your ear will become very itchy, do not poke, prod or push anything into it – this will only make the condition worse in the long term. To prevent swimmer's ear, pour a few drops of alcohol (i.e., surgical spirit, diluted 50:50 with water) into each ear after swimming. Shower, dry, use alcohol drops then allow excess drops to run out of ear onto a towel – the rest will evaporate. (N.B. Although using al-

7

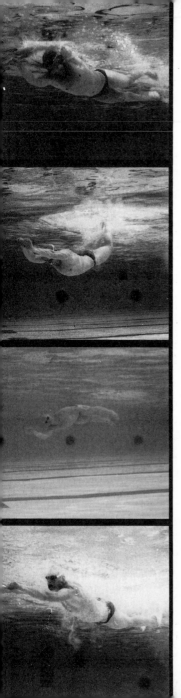

cohol on the ear is commonplace in swimming it is sometimes not looked upon favourably by the medical profession. Do not start using it without consulting your doctor first.)

Skin

As far as possible allow your skin to adjust by itself. However, if dry patches develop then rather than using moisturising cream *after* swimming, use an oil based cream or petroleum jelly *before* swimming. If a skin complaint persists, consult your doctor.

Hair

Not that I know much about it (!) but I'm told that if you wear a cap it will help to protect your hair against chlorine. There are also some special shampoos for swimmers.

Equipment

Swimsuits

There are two popular materials, Lycra and nylon. Lycra swimsuits are stretchy and therefore comfortable; however, chlorine tends to rot the material so they may not last long. If you buy a Lycra swimsuit and want to get the best wear out of it, I suggest you rinse your suit thoroughly after using it. As Lycra is stretchy and clings when it is wet, it doesn't tend to be baggy in the water and therefore makes a good racing swimsuit.

Nylon has little stretch and does not fit as well as Lycra, but the material has much more tolerance to chlorine. However, this does not mean you should not rinse it thoroughly after use for extended life.

Goggles

Goggles have made a huge difference to swimming. Not only do they prevent the eyes from becoming irritated from chlorine and bad pH balance, but they have also made swimming training more interesting. In addition to this, being able to see when you are in the water enables you to feel more comfortable and relaxed which, of course, will enable

9

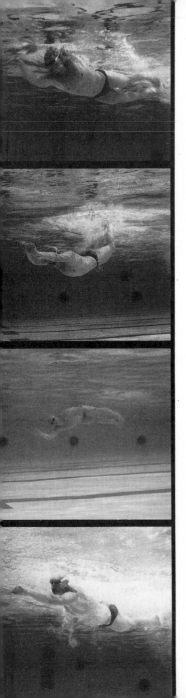

you to improve your technique.

Which are the right goggles for you? Unfortunately, due to the different configurations of people's faces, it is usually a question of trial and error to find out which size goggles suit you best. It often follows, however, that people with deep-set eyes suit small goggles, while those with wide-set eyes find that bigger goggles seem to work better. If your goggles leak regularly, check the nose strap is adjusted to suit you and try wearing the elastic strap higher on the back of your head. If this fails to stop the leaking, I suggest you try a different size of goggles.

Just because your goggles fit, don't expect to be able to dive into the pool with them staying on. It takes many years of experience to be able to dive in without them at least leaking, and even experienced swimmers find that occasionally they will come off. I suggest you do not dive wearing goggles, because of the risk of damage to your eyes.

If you have trouble with your goggles fogging up, try licking the inside and then rinsing them quickly. If this fails there is some anti-mist liquid you can buy, and even anti-mist goggles.

There are many different shades and tints for goggles. I have no recommendations to make unless you are swimming outdoors in a hot country with lots of sunshine – if this is the case wear dark-tinted goggles.

10

Caps

Swimming caps have two roles, both of which are useless to me! Firstly, they protect the hair against chlorine and bad pH balance in the water. Secondly, they cut down resistance in the water made by hair. A cap can also help where bad ear problems are persistent by stopping some of the water entering the ear. However, it would have to be used in conjunction with ear plugs to be really effective. Caps are made from a rubber base and are therefore susceptible to rotting if not dried properly and powdered with talc.

Kickboards

Kickboards should have plenty of buoyancy and be large enough to lean on comfortably. If you can, avoid polystyrene. It will soon start to flake and, apart from being messy around the house, the flakes can also cause problems with swimming-pool filters.

Pull buoys

Pull buoys can come in all sorts of shapes and sizes, and are designed to be held between your thighs to give your legs buoyancy while pulling only. As with kickboards, try to keep away from polystyrene. My particular preference is for the type made in two sections joined together by nylon cord. I find them not only easier to keep in place, but also, when turning, less likely to cause injury.

11

In the Water

'Feel'

If you intend to be a good swimmer, then perhaps 'feel' for the water is the most important factor. Let me try and explain with an example: walking. As you put your foot on the ground, you feel it underneath your foot. If you do not feel the ground giving under your foot, you pick up your other foot ready to make another step. In all the swimming strokes you place the palm of your hand in the water and 'press' a handful of water, as you would the rung of a ladder. Once you have a good 'hold', you pull your body past your hand. The trick of swimming is in getting such a grip on the water that, just as in the case of climbing a ladder, your hand stays on the rung or, in swimming, at the same point in the water, and you 'lever' your body past your hand. So the more sensitive you are to the 'feel' of your 'hold' on the water, the less likelihood there is of your hand slipping through it.

Relaxation and comfort

Unfortunately, there is no substitute for time spent in the water – the more time you spend in the water the more relaxed and comfortable you become with it.

This is the very reason why occasional swimmers find swimming so tiring. Because they are not relaxed, they tend to use not only the muscles needed to swim but also all the other muscle groups in their body, and consequently become tired extremely quickly.

To help yourself become more comfortable with the water I suggest you imagine yourself lying completely relaxed, fully stretched out on your bed – the water is very similar; it gives you support from underneath. When you start to move your body through the water, make your actions as floppy and relaxed as possible, therefore exerting as little effort as possible. The use of swimming goggles can help you feel more comfortable and at ease with the water.

Hand position

Your hand, in most cases, plays the largest role in propelling you through the water (with perhaps the exception of breaststroke, where lower legs and feet can be just as important).

For the most part, your hands should be pulling directly away (i.e., at 180 degrees) from the far end of the pool – after all, that is the direction you are trying to go! Although this sounds obvious, it does not always happen. For example, in front crawl, if you do not pull down the centreline of your body but much wider, that is down the side of your body, you will tend to compensate

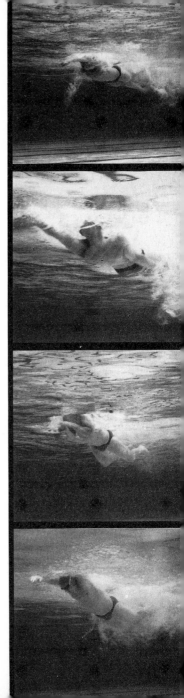

13

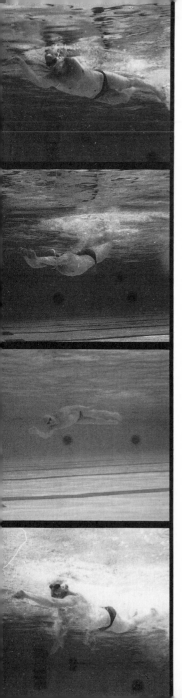

by sloping your hands slightly inwards.

The only other time when the hands will deviate from the 180-degree line to the end of the pool is during the breaststroke pull (see page 37). So, if you concentrate on keeping your hands in the right position, your stroke will automatically come together. What is the right position? For details on technique, read on!

Finger position

The popular belief is that the fingers should be kept tightly together; however, it does require the use of muscles to keep the fingers together. This use of an extra muscle group is unnecessary, because if the finger muscles are kept fairly relaxed, then the fingers will be only a little apart. I feel the gap between the fingers is so small that water will not be able to get through it quick enough, and the additional 'spread' effectively gives the hand more purchase power on the water.

Freestyle

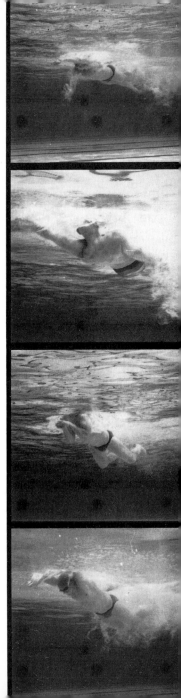

Front crawl, or freestyle as it is called in competition, is the fastest of the swimming strokes and the one on which most top swimmers predominantly train.

Freestyle pull

I will concentrate on the classic technique which most swimmers use. Some top sprinters deviate slightly from this style so they can get a quicker turnover, but let's not concern ourselves with that. This method is not exactly the most attractive stroke.

It is easy to believe that freestyle is swum in a windmill fashion – arms straight out and rotating at a constant speed. Notice in the 'flicker' photographs of me swimming freestyle that as my hand enters the water I take my time to get a good grip before pulling. In the meantime the other hand is actually catching up.

If you turn each page and look at the photographs carefully, you will notice that my hand follows an invisible centreline that runs down the middle of my body. But that's not surprising. If you think about it, if you don't pull down that centreline, then you'll be pulling

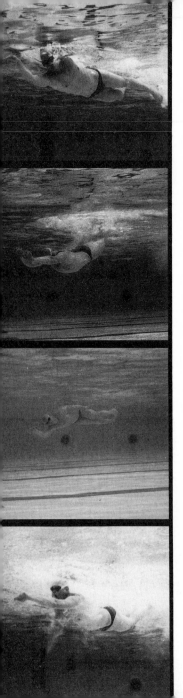

your body away from the direction you want to go.

Let's go back to the beginning of the stroke. As you put your hand in the water, reach as far forward as possible. After all, this is only common sense – the closer you can put your hand to where you're going, the quicker you will get there.

The next movement is the delicate one of getting hold of the water ready to pull. It comes from the fingertips slightly bending and pressing down, and then through to the hand until you have a good 'hold' on the water. Your next movement is a bend of the elbow, which begins the pull. From the point where the arm is straight and the hand becomes level with the elbow, the pull is not particularly strong. However, this is an extremely important part of the stroke – it is when you are gaining control. Once your hand becomes level with your elbow then you start pulling or levering with not only your arm but also your shoulder, and of course this gives you more power in your pull. From the point where your hand becomes level with your elbow, try and keep horizontal to the direction you are going in. By doing this, of course, you are using not only your hand to propel yourself, but also your forearm. This should continue all the way down the centreline of your body until you have to start stretching your arm to finish the

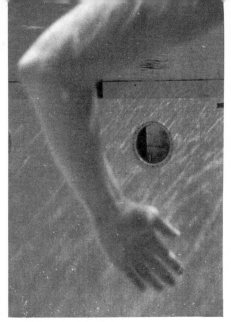

Right position – elbow high. In this position your forearm helps the pull

Wrong position – elbow dropped, so you lose the benefit of your forearm in the pull

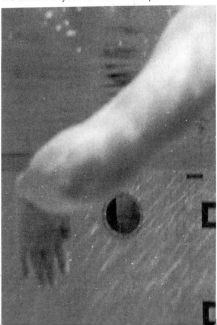

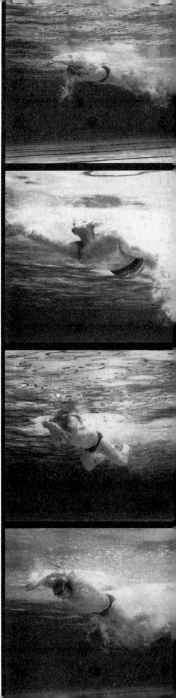

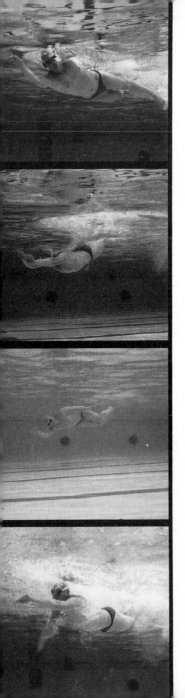

stroke. To make the most of your free-style pull, it is very important to ensure that your arm straightens at the end of the stroke. But don't stop there – allow your hand to continue working all the way down until it is straight in line with your arm. At this point in your stroke your hand will be travelling so fast that it will flick past your leg, and you will have finished the pull cycle.

Breathing

Swimming is unique in that it is about the only sport that requires coordinated breathing. With other sports you can pretty much breathe when you like; with swimming, of course, you can only breathe when your head is above the water. This, for some people, is easy; however there are a few people who will always find this tremendously difficult.

As you travel forward, your head makes a kind of furrow in the water and creates a gully just to the left and right of your ears. To breathe, just rotate your head round and breathe out of the little gully. Note well that the air you already have in your lungs should be exhaled very forcibly a split second *before* your mouth breaks surface. It is also import-ant not to move your head up or down, or from side to side, for reasons men-tioned later. You may wonder which side you should breathe on. There is no correct side, but you probably will find that one side is easier than the other. The

Breathing from the gully

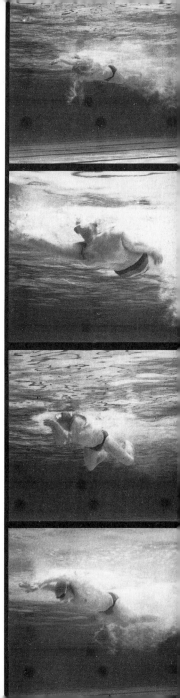

reason for this is that most people have a difference in flexibility in their neck. The more flexible side is usually the one you will feel more comfortable breathing on.

If you are having trouble with your freestyle breathing and you are not wearing goggles, try wearing a pair (see page 9).

If you want to improve the look of your stroke then I suggest you try bilateral breathing. This is simply breathing at every third arm pull in the freestyle cycle – once to your left, once to your right, etc. By breathing bilaterally you are balancing your stroke and making it more even. The rhythm is pull, pull, pull, breathe.

Body positioning

Before we move on to the recovery I would like to cover one point, and that is the positioning of the body. Everybody

has a different buoyancy, and therefore will lie at a different level in the water. Perhaps the most important part is getting the position of your head correct. Your head weighs about 5 kilograms: if you lift it too high you will find your body angle will be changed; conversely, if you have your head too low in the water then your backside will stick up! If you try and keep the water level just a couple of inches above your eyebrows, you will find your body will automatically adopt the right position.

As the head is so crucial to the body position, be careful not to move it unnecessarily. Every movement will affect the position of the body in the water.

Recovery

It is undoubtedly true that what happens under the water is far more important than what happens on top. However, there are some important points I would like to mention about the recovery, which is the carry forward of the head and arm over the water.

All too often I see swimmers lifting their hands out of the water at the end of the pull and swinging the arm round the side of their body, and eventually to the front, ready to take another stroke. In this movement they use almost every muscle in their arm. The key to a good recovery is to use the least effort possible, so the moment you have finished your pull, lift your elbow rather than your hand, keeping the whole lower arm and hand as relaxed and loose as possible. Bring your elbow up and allow your lower arm to be carried forward almost as if it were a puppet's arm. Of course, if you do not lift your elbow high enough your hand will drag in the water, or you could cheat by swinging your arm in a high arc and consequently slip into the mistake of picking your hand up rather than your elbow.

Do not be in too much of a hurry to swim fast. Just get the stroke right, and the speed will look after itself.

Drills

There are three exercises you can do to help your freestyle pull.

1. *Catch-up (flicker sequence E)*

Catch-up freestyle is literally what it says it is. You do not start your pull until the recovering hand actually touches the hand in the water waiting to pull. So if you were lying in the water with your arms stretched in front of you and you pulled with your left hand, you would not start to pull again with your right hand until it had been touched by your left hand. This drill gives you lots of time to concentrate on the feel for the water and getting a good handhold on it. It also gives you time to stretch at the beginning of the stroke, and finally it

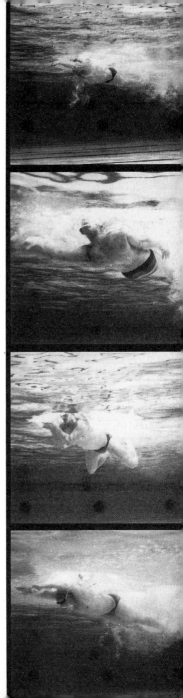

21

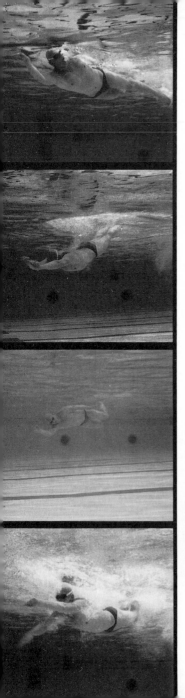

also encourages you to complete the pull properly.

2. *Water polo*

Water polo is simply swimming freestyle with your head out of the water. Try and keep your head completely still – imagine a cup of water on your head and try not to spill a drop. As you put your hand into the water check your elbows do not drop, and make sure you finish your pull. The objects of the water polo drill are to make sure 1) that your head does not move around, 2) that your elbows do not drop, and 3) that your hand enters the water in the correct position. On top of those benefits it also,

Water polo

22

being difficult, builds up the muscles needed to swim freestyle and it forces you to kick very hard and deep in order to keep your upper body high.

3. *Chicken wing*

To swim chicken wing, you pull underwater as normal in freestyle. At the end of your stroke put your thumb on your thigh and draw it up the side of your body, under the underside of your armpit, touching your ear, and then on into the front of the freestyle pull. Throughout this whole movement the elbow must be lifted as high as possible in order to keep your thumb on the side of your body. It is also necessary to relax

Chicken wing drill seen from above

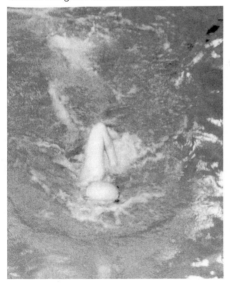

23

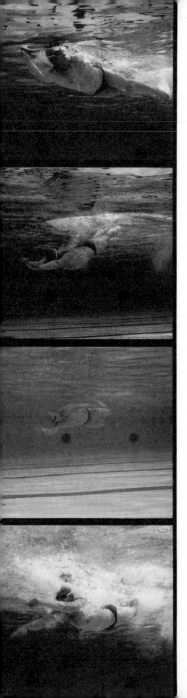

the lower arm completely. These are the benefits: to ensure you have a high elbow in your recovery, and also to try and relax your forearm and hands.

There are many other drills you can use, but I think these are the most important in helping you achieve a good-looking and efficient freestyle.

Land exercises

Freestyle is broken down very much into two different disciplines: sprinting and long-distance swimming. The sprinter needs to be more explosive, so any land training he does should concentrate on that; while the long-distance swimmer needs to have endurance and stamina.

The best way to help your freestyle pull outside the water is to do weight-training and circuit training. Sprinters need to concentrate more on heavier weights to build up strength, although they should not ignore circuit training, which will help to give them the endurance to take them through to the end of their race. Likewise, long-distance swimmers should not ignore heavy weight-training as a way of improving their speed and keeping a balance to their body. See pages 83-96 for exercise suggestions.

Freestyle kick

When you first start to learn how to swim, especially if you are younger, you tend to try a normal running action in the water. This bending of the knees destroys the forward propulsion you are trying to create with your legs.

You need to keep your legs fairly straight while you are kicking freestyle, and your ankles completely loose. The drive from the hip along a straightish leg to a fully flexed ankle is actually what propels you in freestyle kick.

There are four types of kick: two beat, four beat, six beat, and cross-over. They represent the number of kicks to each full arm cycle of two pulls. A two-beat kick is a very slow kick, which is more suitable to some long-distance swimmers. A six-beat kick, however, is a fast kick which is more suitable to sprinters. It goes without saying that the more kick you put in each cycle of your stroke, the more propulsion you will get out of your legs.

The final category, cross-over, is seldom, if ever, actually taught. It seems to develop naturally with some swimmers, even world-class competitors. When they breathe, in order to balance the stroke, they cross their legs over in between kicks. If you *naturally* adopt this rhythm and are moving smoothly, don't change it!

Drills

There are no drills that I would particularly recommend for freestyle kick. However, I would strongly recommend

25

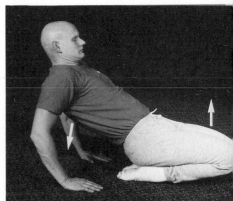

Rock back on your ankles

kicking with a board. When you kick with a board, time yourself regularly and try and improve on yourself.

Flexibility exercises

As I have explained earlier on, freestyle kick relies on a flipper-type movement of the ankle. So the more flexible your ankles are, the more effective your freestyle leg kick will be. In particular, it relies on how much you can flex the foot at the ankle.

1. Put a towel down on the floor, folded many times, and kneel down sitting on your ankles. Gently start leaning further back until the only part of your body left on the ground is the front of your feet. You will find that this will gradually increase ankle flexibility.

2. Fold a towel many times and put it on the ground. Put your foot into the

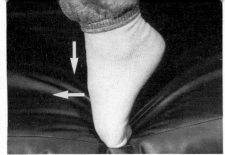

Push down and forward on your toes

towel with your toes bunched up and push against your toes in much the same way as a ballet dancer would.

In a gym, of course, use the exercise mats instead of the towel.

Land exercises

You should work at anything that can strengthen your legs, such as running and cycling. Two more suggestions are as follows:

1. Lie on your back with your hands palms down under your buttocks. Lift your legs as if kicking backstroke. Do not allow your legs to hit the ground.

2. A similar exercise to the previous one, this time lie on your stomach with your arms extended in front of you and kick with knees off the ground. But be careful not to bend too much at the knee. It is basically a straight leg action.

As I have mentioned in the 'Pull' section, there are two categories of freestyle: sprinters and long distance. So bear in mind the same considerations as you would do for freestyle pull.

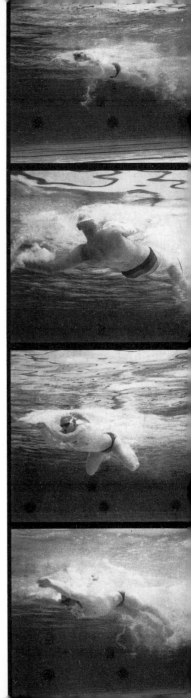

Backstroke

Backstroke pull

Just as with freestyle pull, many people think that backstroke pull is similar to a windmill action. Although backstroke does not have quite such a catch-up motion, one hand catching up with the other hand at the beginning of the stroke, there is a definite hesitation at the beginning of the pull as the hand takes a 'hold' of the water. Furthermore, although the arms are straight while out of the water, they should not be straight underwater.

Let me take you stage by stage through a backstroke pull cycle. First, put your little finger in the water above your head. The fact that you are putting your little finger in first ensures your hand will be in the correct position

Try putting your little finger in first

The bent arm in press position

ready to start a backstroke pull. You should start pulling from your fingertips, so your hand gets in the right position to get a decent grip on the water. After it has got a handful of water, the first movement is from the elbow. Bend it, and bring your hand in line with your elbow as in freestyle. The backstroke pull now becomes more of a press. Keep your hand in line with your elbow as long as you can throughout the backstroke press. The combination of your hand and forearm gives you more surface area pressing against the water in order to move you forwards.

When your elbow reaches the bottom of your ribs, it is impossible to keep your hand along the same horizontal line. It is then a question of continuing to press down until your hand touches your leg, and even then you should not stop until

29

the arm and the hand are completely straightened. A good way of practising this is to allow your fingers to actually touch your leg. Of course, this gives you a chance to actually feel whether or not you have got your whole arm straight and in the right position.

Having said all that, perfecting the correct backstroke technique is not easy by any means. It is not just a question of bending the elbow at the right time; what you must do to help yourself is to roll your body. As you put your little finger in the water and start your pull, let your opposite shoulder come out of the water until it is literally pointing towards the ceiling. By the time this has happened your hand will be level with your elbow, and the fact that your opposite shoulder has rotated round will mean that the elbow is far deeper than if your body was flat with the water. Otherwise, you would not be able to bend your elbow to a 90 degree angle without the hand pulling along the surface of the water or even out of the water. The shoulder roll not only helps the pull, it also helps the recovery of backstroke. As you roll your shoulder it makes it easier to get the recovering arm and hand out of the water.

As with all strokes, it is important to keep the head still. Any unnecessary movement of the head will cause movement in the body. As your mouth is always out of the water, there is no

30

reason to move the head at all during the stroke cycle. It is important not to keep your head too far out of the water as it not only needs quite a lot of strength and effort to do this, but it also makes your body sink and sag in the middle. Although your face is not underwater while you are swimming backstroke, I suggest you wear goggles to protect your eyes from the splashes of water that tend to upset occasional swimmers.

As you are swimming backstroke, allow your head to lean back so that the water is as high as possible without coming over the top of your head and interfering with your breathing. As a general hint, it is a good idea to look slightly ahead of you at the ceiling.

As you are swimming it is inevitable that there is a considerable amount of splash. Although you can breathe at any time during the cycle of backstroke, there is a time that most top backstrokers prefer. This moment is when the hand is directly above the head. The reasoning behind this is that

Try breathing when the hand is above the head

the hand which is doing the pulling has been in the water long enough for any splash it created entering the water to have subsided, and any splash from the recovering arm has not reached the mouth at that point.

Drills

1. One-armed backstroke

One-armed backstroke is exactly what it says it is. It is backstroke swum using only one arm. For the sake of this example, let's say that your left arm is kept with your hand against your thigh. The right arm is used just as if you are swimming the full stroke. Let us now run through the movement of the right arm. The hand is put in the water, little finger first; the catch happens. The catch is unlike butterfly and freestyle, but similar to breaststroke – the hand makes the first significant move. At this point the left shoulder is rolled up to face the ceiling. This roll enables the right hand to pull deeper in the water and therefore the resulting pull is more effective. The next part of the stroke comes from keeping your arm straight above your head and rotating it in an arc until your hand passes your elbow. At this point the press begins – you are pressing on your hand rather than pulling. The press continues until the arm is straight and the hand slaps against your thigh.

One-armed backstroke is a very effective drill for making you conscious of

Shoulder facing the ceiling

two important facts. One of these is that the hand in backstroke goes through more movement than in any other stroke. Just before finishing the stroke, the hand should nearly be at right angles to the forearm. Because the depth of your hand is affected so much by the shoulder roll, whether or not your shoulder is facing towards the ceiling, one-armed backstroke also ensures you become more conscious of how deep in the water your hand is. Obviously, the deeper your hand is in the water, the more efficient and more effective your pull is – more of your pull, or press, is pressing forward rather than forcing your body sideways.

2. Double-armed backstroke
Double-armed backstroke is similar to swimming butterfly on your back, re-

33

taining the backstroke kick. The result of swimming backstroke with both arms together is that you are unable to roll your shoulder, and therefore it is difficult to get your hands deep into the water. This means you tend to pull air. The main point of double-armed backstroke is to concentrate on getting your arms as low as possible in the water. To achieve this you have to go into the press position; there is no other way. Therefore, this drill makes you more conscious of the flexibility in your shoulder joints. There are two main focuses of concentration: your hands, and how close together you can get your elbows underneath yourself halfway through the stroke (you should feel your shoulder blades touching together in the middle of your back).

Land exercises

As, with backstroke, it is important to get your elbow as deep as possible in the water, it is worth spending more time on shoulder mobility.

There is one particular land exercise I would like to recommend for backstroke: the bench dip. Get a chair, sit down on a bench with the chair in front of you, put your feet up on the chair, take hold of the bench with both your hands, and lower your body down to the floor and back up again. This strengthens and stretches your shoulders for backstroke.

34

Backstroke kick

Backstroke kick is very like freestyle in action. The main part of the kick is in the ankles, and it is important that they remain floppy and relaxed. Of course, the real difference is that the main part of the kick is in the upward stroke rather than the downward stroke of freestyle. The other marked difference is the fact that on backstroke you do not breathe to one side, and therefore there is no need to stabilize the body as you do on freestyle. However, because of the shoulder rotation, it is necessary to use the kick as a balancing force whilst you are swimming.

The rate of kick during the stroke really depends on what your preference is, and on the distance you are swimming.

Drills

The main drill for all the other strokes for kick is kicking with a board. However, while kicking backstroke the body automatically sits at the same level as it would do while you're swimming; therefore you will not need the help of a kickboard.

1. *Kicking*

Although there is no need to kick with a board, it is a good idea to kick with your arms outstretched above your head. While you are doing this

kicking, time yourself and make a mental note of what you are doing differently to achieve a faster time.

2. *Kicking on your side*

The most effective drill you can do for kick is undoubtedly backstroke on your side. Extend your bottom arm forward, hold your top arm backwards close to the body, and kick on your side. The object of this drill is to strengthen the leg kick through the whole motion of the kick. When normally kicking backstroke, your legs on the upward motion break the surface and therefore are not worked through the full motion of the kick. Make sure you do the same distance on either side of your body – you don't want to be so strong on one side that you swim round in circles!

Flexibility

Once more, the exercises needed for freestyle leg kick have the same benefit for backstroke leg kick. When referring to the freestyle section on land exercises look at the advice for sprinters as this will be particularly beneficial.

The final bit of advice which I have for you is to do with turns. Every time you approach your turn concentrate on exactly how far it is from the warning flags to the wall – you should practise to have it down to a fine art. You can then consider yourself a good backstroke turner. It is difficult, but necessary.

Breaststroke

Breaststroke pull

Breaststroke is the most inefficient of all the strokes, and therefore is one of the hardest ones to swim in competition. The main difference between breaststroke and the other strokes is the fact that the recovery is done underwater. On top of this there are three main types of pull you can do in breaststroke. It has only been possible in this book to picture one of these styles, and that is the one I practise. I will cover the other techniques of swimming breaststroke quickly, by comparing them with the one in sequence C.

1. *Elbows up*

The beginning of the pull is exactly the same as the one pictured; however, where it differs is on the beginning of the recovery. Instead of squeezing your elbows together, keep your elbows up. The idea is to keep your elbows as still as possible and allow your hands to do the work.

2. *Pull down the centre*

This technique differs completely from the one pictured. In fact it is much more similar to butterfly. So, follow the in-

structions for butterfly until your hands are level with your shoulders, and then pull your hands up slightly. Rotate your hands round so that they are pointing in the direction you are going, and gently push them forward until they are ready for another stroke cycle.

3. *Breaststroke squeeze*

This is by far the most common form of breaststroke pull. In fact, most of the top breaststrokers use it, and I personally recommend that you try this method first before moving on to any others. Start with your arms stretched out in front of you, and rotate your hands around so they are facing back to back and touching. Stretch out as far as you can in front of you. As you are lying in the water with stretched-out arms it's easy to stretch just the arms and not the rest of your body. The stretch should not only include your arms but also your shoulders. When you are stretching your arms out, allow your shoulders to curl round until they are almost touching your ears – this will give you a couple of inches extra reach, which of course will help you get to the end faster.

Once you are in this totally stretched position you are ready to start your pull. Begin with your fingertips pulling round so your hands get a nice hold on the water. Then pull along just below the surface of the water with straight arms.

One of the problems with

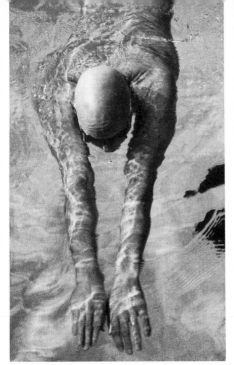

Stretched out as far as possible with rounded shoulders

breaststroke is knowing when to stop pulling. Because the recovery of breaststroke pull is underwater, it is extremely hard to get your hands back into the position needed to start another pull. The further back you pull, the harder it is to get them back into the start position. So the trick is judging the right time. The key is in hand position. If you begin your stroke with your hands, then once they are facing the end of the pool you should start your recovery. Unfortunately, at this point it feels as though your body is falling forward in

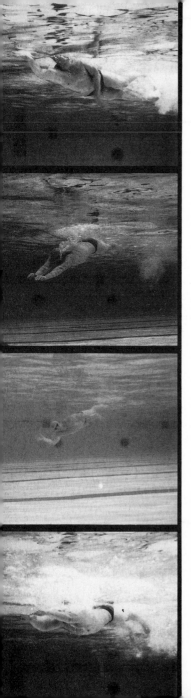

the water and therefore it becomes a temptation to continue pulling. As a very approximate guide, the arms should travel through about a 45-degree arc. Once you have reached this point in your pull you have finished the pull cycle.

Where this technique differs from the other two techniques is that instead of finishing the pull here, you carry it on by allowing your hands to rotate round – trying to keep the handful of water in your hands until your palms are facing each other. Then start pushing your palms until they are nearly together. At this point, start squeezing your elbows together and pulling your hands up towards your chin. What you are trying to do is form a kind of funnel between your hands, elbows and body. By squeezing your elbows together you are forcing the water down through the funnel and out past your elbows. Of course this, although not strictly part of the pull, helps continue pushing you forward.

At this point you will be ready to start the recovery. As I have mentioned before, the recovery is done underwater and therefore is far more tiring than the recovery on other strokes. When I start pushing my hands forward towards the start position of the stroke, I tilt my hands round so the palms of my hands face towards the bottom of the pool. I try to do this as early as possible in the recovery, in order to keep myself high in the water. This, however, is very much a personal preference. Many breaststrokers prefer to keep their palms facing each other until the arms are fully extended before then rotating them round ready to start another pull. I don't like letting my body sink, so I try and keep my body as high as possible in the water at all times during a stroke cycle. By turning your palms down towards the bottom you can maintain a slight pressure pushing downwards, and therefore keep your body position high in the water. I believe this is particularly important for a sprinter, so he can increase his turnover.

Finally, if you leave your palms together until you are ready to start your pull, there is a temptation to begin it before you have rotated your hands and arms around. This would mean you would lose part of it. You can, of course, begin your pull too early, even if your palms are facing the bottom of the pool; however, because they only have to turn through 90 degrees there is less likelihood of losing quite so much off the pull.

With all the other strokes, it is easy to know when to stop pulling (working to move forward) – when your hands come out of the water you have stopped your pull. In breaststroke, because your hands do not come out of the water, you must be very careful not to continue

your pull (working) when you are just trying to recover your arms back to the starting position. After I have got a good hold on the water, I pull as hard as I possibly can until my hands are facing the back of the pool. At this point I relax totally, and the rest of the pull (the squeeze) I use the speed at which my arms are moving and just redirect them. It is this ability to relax at the end of the pull that will enable you to swim with less effort.

To breathe on breaststroke, as with all the other strokes, it is best to keep your head as still as possible. Some people will find it possible to breathe on breaststroke without moving their head at all; however, others will find it necessary to tilt the head slightly upwards at the critical point. As you start your pull, by tilting your palms very slightly down towards the bottom of the pool you make it possible to use your arms to lever your body upwards, therefore making it possible to breathe. This, in my opinion, should be done early on in the stroke cycle. Beware, when you are trying to swim breaststroke flat out, of the temptation to duck your head into the water at the end of the pull. This can cause your breaststroke to become very jerky.

Drills

It is a good idea to swim a considerable amount of breaststroke with a 'pull

42

buoy' using predominantly your arms. However, it is difficult and I suggest that you cheat a little by using just a slight butterfly leg kick at the point where you would normally kick on breaststroke. I believe without this butterfly leg kick during this drill, you will not achieve the right position to simulate a proper breaststroke pull. (A dolphin leg kick is the butterfly leg kick – the undulation of the bottom half of the body that you can see in the photographs of the butterfly.)

1. *Breaststroke pull, freestyle leg kick*

This is exactly what it says it is – you swim a breaststroke pull and instead of kicking breaststroke do a freestyle leg kick. This drill enables you to work your arms without getting quite the same propulsion from your legs. This makes you work harder with your arms. It is also possible, because you are not waiting for your legs at the beginning of each stroke, to pull quicker than you would do while you are swimming breaststroke.

2. *Submarine breaststroke (flicker sequence F)*

This is the most popular drill for top breaststrokers. It is breaststroke with a little dolphin leg kick, forcing your body under water. You kick a regular breaststroke kick, and then bob under the water using a butterfly-style kick. Once under water, stretch forward (con-

43

centrating on that stretch discussed earlier). Lift your hands slightly above the point you would normally, and start an ordinary pull. However, because you are underwater and need to reach the surface, you must squeeze your elbows together a little more to get you to the surface. Do not, however, pull past where you would do when you are swimming breaststroke normally. While you are doing this drill, concentrate on stretching as far forward as possible at the beginning of the stroke so you are getting every inch that you can.

Land exercises

Weight-training and circuit training are the best forms of strengthening your arms for the breaststroke pull. While circuit training will give you slightly more endurance, heavy weight-training will give you the strength you need for breaststroke pull. You need to concentrate on your triceps (the back of your upper arm) and your laterals (the muscle running down the back side of your armpit). Dips are particularly good for developing your triceps (dips are usually done on parallel bars which are just over a shoulder-width wide; a dip is simply lowering your body up and down without touching the floor). While doing dips, try to ensure that in the down position your elbow at least makes the 90-degree angle. To strengthen your lats, use the lat machine

44

which most gyms have. It is usually the machine which has a bar suspended some 7 feet in the air for you to hold and pull down. I suggest you do this in a sitting position with your hands as far apart as possible on the bar, and pull down so the bar touches the back of your neck rather than the front of your chest. By doing it this way round, you will concentrate more on your lats.

Flexibility exercises

As breaststroke pull develops your triceps and lateral muscles it is important to concentrate on them when considering flexibility. The best way of achieving this is to put your hand behind your head and down your back; with your other hand, take hold of your elbow and pull it across. By doing this you will successfully stretch your lats.

45

However, to successfully stretch the triceps it may be necessary to get some help. Put your left hand behind your head and push it down your back. The person helping you should take hold of your wrist and gently push it across towards your left shoulder. In his other hand, he then takes hold of your elbow and pulls it gently across to your right shoulder. I should emphasize that this must be done extremely carefully so you do not hurt yourself. Before starting, agree with the person helping you that he should stop stretching you when you say stop. (For more information about stretching, turn to page 83).

Breaststroke legs

You will see by flicking through the book that the kick on breaststroke is very similar to a frog's. This movement is not always possible for some people. Stand up with your legs together. Put your weight on the back of your heels and try to turn your feet outwards, keeping your legs together. If your feet go to the position 9 to 3 without your legs coming apart or your knees bending, then you should find breaststroke kick very easy. If your feet go to the position 10 to 2, then breaststroke should be easy also. If your feet will only go to the position 11 to 1 then the kick will be more difficult for you. If you cannot move your feet from twelve o'clock, or perhaps not even be able to get them properly into twelve o'clock because you are pigeon-toed, then you will never be able to kick proper breaststroke. However, you may be able to improve the possibility of swimming breaststroke kick by working on the flexibility of your knees and ankles (see pages 83-93).

Starting in the stretched-out position with your legs together and your toes pointed, lift your heels up towards your backside. I find it sometimes helps to keep your heels gently touched together while pulling your feet up. As your feet come up, allow your knees to drift apart. The body should remain as straight as possible down to the knees, but it is all too easy to allow them to come up towards the body. This means that all the water rushing past your body will hit your knees and therefore slow you down. And this is where, by touching your heels together, you can concentrate on lifting your heels up rather than dropping your knees forward.

Once your heels are nearly touching your backside, pull your feet up and rotate them around, as if from the little toe, as far apart as possible. At this point the inside of your foot should be pointing in the opposite direction from the way in which you are going. In fact the whole of the inside of your shin should also be in that position. Because of the difference between people's bodies you may find that, because you are more

47

Breaststroke kick – notice how the feet squeeze
completely together

48

flexible in the knees and ankles than I am, your knees may not need to be so far apart. On the other hand, you may find that you have less flexibility in your knees and ankles than I do, and that your knees will be further apart. But, as a general rule, the closer together your knees are, the more effective your kick will be.

As you set your feet ready to start your kick, you will find them naturally drifting into the position where your heel, knee and hip are on the same line. Kick straight out along that line. After your knees have locked straight, allow your feet to continue on travelling until they are together. You may find it helpful to touch your big toes together. This last little squeeze cannot be achieved by just the lower part of your leg. It really comes from trying to clamp your knees together, which only happens after you have straightened them. Once your toes have touched together, you begin a new cycle of your stroke by touching your heels together and pulling up your legs again.

Drills

The legs play a larger overall part in this stroke than in any other stroke, and therefore it is perhaps slightly more important to concentrate on the leg kick. Do lots of kicking with a board, and try to get used to using only the

49

muscle groups required. Kick out – squeeze together – pull up.

1. *Kicking underwater*
Kick three or more times underwater before breathing, and then duck down underwater to continue. While you are underwater, concentrate on squeezing your knees together.

2. *Hands behind your back*
Place your hands behind your back with your thumbs on your backside and kick breaststroke. Concentrate on trying to raise your heels right up to touch your thumbs. This will help you lift your heels straight up behind you, rather than out to the side. Furthermore, in order to breathe you need to finish your kick.

Land exercises

Running and cycling are good ways of conditioning your legs for breaststroke. However, if you play other sports do be careful, as breaststroke makes your knee joints very loose and flexible and therefore prone to slight pulls. Once you have pulled your knee, then the repetitive movement of breaststroke kick can cause your knee to swell up quite badly. This ailment is often known as 'breaststroker's knee'. Many people believe that breaststroker's knee is caused by breaststroke, but I think it is usually caused by a small pull of the tendons or ligaments in the knee outside the water.

50

I suffered one year fairly badly from this as a result of a game of squash. On another occasion I fell down a fire-escape ladder and was left hanging by the knee – one week later I started having problems with breaststroker's knee.

Weight-training and circuit training are also very effective in helping your kick. As the kick on breaststroke is so important, concentrate not only on heavy weight-training but also on circuit training to increase endurance and stamina.

Flexibility

As the knee can give a breaststroke swimmer problems, it is worth making sure that the legs are well warmed up and stretched before swimming. Then take it easy for the first few lengths and build up your speed gradually.

Many breaststroke swimmers concentrate their stretching exercises on the inside of their knee and forget about the side. I suggest you do both exercises shown on pages 90 and 91.

Butterfly

There is no doubt that butterfly is the most 'fish-like' stroke. When swum properly, it feels as though you are floating through the water with each pull flowing smoothly into the next one; however, this fluid motion is not an easy one to achieve.

Butterfly pull

Butterfly is undoubtedly the most difficult stroke to learn. Having said that, once you have mastered it, it is perhaps the most satisfying stroke to swim.

It is indeed the fluid, flowing motion that is rather tricky. In fact, I have an admission to make here – it was not until I was eighteen years old that I learned how to swim butterfly properly. I could not get the hang of putting the stroke together, and brute force wasn't enough. I cheated by swimming breaststroke leg kick with butterfly arm pull, which at the time was not illegal. However, now the competitive regulations state that butterfly should be swum with a dolphin leg kick.

It is not only necessary to allow your body to flow with the rhythm of the stroke, but also there is a need for great flexibility of the shoulders. Because you are raising both arms out of the water at the same time, you cannot cheat, as in freestyle, by rolling your body slightly to one side. There can be two reasons why you do not have the flexibility to swim butterfly:

1. Your tendons and muscle groups around your shoulders and chest are too tight or highly developed. By working on the flexibility of your shoulders you can make it much easier to learn butterfly.

2. Because of the size or position of your scapula (shoulder blades), as you start to raise your elbows out of the water, they hit together in the centre of your shoulders and prevent you from lifting your arms out of the water properly. Unfortunately, the flexibility exercises that I can recommend to you will not cure this problem; it might just make it a little easier for you to swim butterfly. However, having said this, it should not make it impossible for you to swim butterfly – just difficult, but aren't all the things worth doing in life difficult!

The underwater part of butterfly pull is very similar to the movement required to get out of the swimming pool. To pull yourself out of the water, put both hands on the side of the pool a nice comfortable distance apart. Press down on your hands and try to get your elbows level or above your hands. Con-

tinue to press down on your hands until your elbows lock.

As you are stretched out when you are swimming butterfly, you press down on your fingertips until your hands have a good grip on the water. You then pull your hands towards you in the same manner as if you were pulling yourself out of the water. Note that this first movement is achieved by bending the elbows and using the arms rather than the shoulders. This movement differs slightly from pulling your body out of the water, because you can move your hands slightly in the water, where on the side of the pool your hands cannot move at all. As you improve at butterfly, one of the things you should try to achieve is getting a better reach. Stretch your arms out in front of you, but also round your shoulders to gain every inch possible in your reach. As you get better at this, you may find that at the beginning of the stroke your hands tend to be very close together. This will mean that during the first part of the stroke your hands will be pulling slightly outwards to get in line with your shoulders.

Once your hands are level with your elbows, try to use your forearms as well as your hands to pull yourself through the water for as long as possible. Then continue your pull until your elbows and hands are straight. Your hands should be roughly a shoulder-width apart throughout the whole cycle of the

Arms stretched, shoulders rounded

Straighten your arms at the end of the stroke – brush your thumbs against your thighs

stroke; they can be slightly further from your body than if you were pulling yourself out of the water.

Some people do not pull throughout the stroke with their hands a shoulder-width apart. They prefer their hands to follow a club-shaped pattern through the water. The hands pull out slightly till they become level with the shoulders; they then squeeze slightly together until the hands are fairly close and push straight down until they get to the end of the stroke.

There is no right way; find out what suits you best.

55

Butterfly tends to be very tiring, so it's easy to get into the bad habit of not finishing your stroke properly. Brushing your thumbs against your thighs tends to be a good way of reminding yourself to finish properly – straightening your arms at the end of the stroke.

Butterfly recovery differs from freestyle: you must lift your arms not only from your elbows but also your little fingers. In other words, instead of taking your hands out of the water at the back of the stroke and following a line straight to the catch position, you have to bring them round in an arc to the beginning position of the stroke. This, of course, takes more effort.

Try to avoid the temptation of starting the stroke too early. If you put your hands in the water before your arms are stretched forward in line with your shoulders, as they hit the water they will prevent you from going forward. If you manage to get your arms cleanly extended and in line with your shoulders, your hands will punch a hole through the water and allow your body to follow rather than acting as a brake. Perhaps this concept of the body following the hands is the most important part of butterfly, which I will continue to explain under the 'kick' section.

When learning how to swim butterfly, it is a good idea not to try the full stroke first. It is easier to break it down into drills and practise the drills before actually trying the stroke. This differs from other strokes, where the drills act as a way of improving them.

Drills

As I have mentioned butterfly drills will help you to master butterfly. If you can already swim butterfly, as with the other stroke drills, you can use them to perfect your stroke.

1. One-armed butterfly

This drill is very similar to freestyle catch-up, covered in an earlier section. It is literally what it says it is – swimming butterfly with one arm – but don't panic, it's not as hard as it sounds. Before attempting this drill, have a go at swimming catch-up freestyle. Once you have mastered that, instead of kicking freestyle, just add a slight butterfly leg kick in between each stroke. As your hands touch together each time, angle your hands down and allow your body to flow slightly underwater. When you begin the pull, direct your body towards the surface again. When you first start this, exaggerate the movement so you travel under the water a fair way. Once you get the hang of it, you can cut down the amount of duck under the water to a minimum. Try to concentrate on keeping very relaxed and loose with a nice, flowing rhythm. As with catch-up, you should breathe on the side in much the same way as in freestyle. This drill can

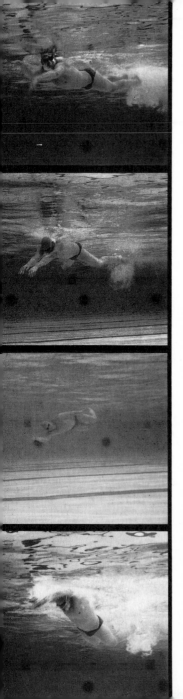

also be done just with one arm – swimming a whole length just using, say, the left arm, and then coming back with the right arm.

As you progress with this one-armed drill, once in a while try adding a full stroke (sequence H). Slowly work down to doing one to the left, one to the right, and one double. Keep building on this exercise until you can do several double-arm pulls to one or two single-arm pulls, and eventually you will slip into the full stroke.

Land exercises

The last 25 per cent of the pull on butterfly is probably more important than in any other stroke. If it is not finished properly, then it is impossible to achieve that fluid motion I have been mentioning. To help yourself with this movement, you can attempt to build up your tricep muscles (the muscle at the back of your arm).

Parallel bars are a piece of apparatus used in a gym: two adjustable bars parallel to the ground. Jump up onto the parallel bars so your hands are stretched out down beside you, and supporting your weight. Lower yourself slowly down until your elbows are at a 90-degree angle, and then slowly straighten your arms again.

Of course, not everybody has parallel bars in their back room, so I suggest doing the same exercise but with chairs.

Get three chairs and put two a hip's width apart. Put the other in front of these chairs, facing them. Place your hands on the two chairs a hip's width apart, and raise your legs and put them on the chair that is in front of you. Make sure the chairs you use will not tip as you put your weight on them. Once you have your weight on your arms and suspended between the chairs, bend your elbows and allow your body to go down towards the floor until your backside nearly touches the ground. Then push down and straighten your elbows. Start off with, say, 10 of these dips. Each day add an extra set of 10 until you get to 6 sets of 10. Once you have achieved this, your next goal is to do 60 straight. If you are really keen, 3 sets of 60 should really help you!

Apart from the dips, the most important part of land training for butterfly is weight-training and circuit training. As even the 200-metre butterfly has turned into basically a sprint, concentrate not only on the circuit training but on heavy weights.

Butterfly kick

Butterfly leg kick is simply an undulation which runs through your whole body. The competitive regulations state that your feet should be together while swimming butterfly kick, so this prohibits breaststroke kick.

It is important to control your leg

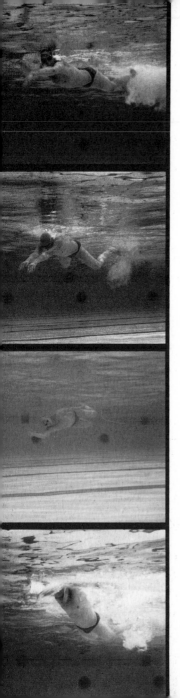

kick while you are swimming butterfly, but in controlling it you must not make it too mechanical. Remember, as a general rule, the legs are following through what the upper body has just done. Obviously, as you master the supple movements, you can start working your legs while you are swimming without upsetting the flowing movements of butterfly. This will come with practice

If you are just lying in the water trying to kick butterfly, dip your hands down in the water and up again, and allow that ripple to go through your body from top to bottom. The actual power comes from the flip of your feet at the end of the ripple. To achieve this movement, you must stay relaxed in the water and allow not only your arms to move, but also your back and your hips, and then down through your knees to your feet. If you are trying the kick only, don't hesitate to overexaggerate it in order to get the feel for it. You may now understand why it is that butterfly leg kick is often known as dolphin leg kick, and 'butterfly' goes under the name of 'dolphin'. However, now swimmers tend to abbreviate 'butterfly' to 'fly'.

Drills

1. *Duck dive*
As I have already mentioned, it is worth getting to know exactly what you are

60

trying to do in butterfly, and this can be achieved by starting the kick with your hands and allowing the undulation to flow through your body. This can be exaggerated to the point where it is literally a duck dive in between each undulation. Lie in the water, duck down hard and then arch your body up towards the surface and breathe, followed by another duck down under the water.

2. *Fly kick on your side (flicker sequence G)*

This is simply kicking on your side, with the top arm down to your side and the bottom arm (the arm deepest in the water) stretched out in front of you. To breathe, use your bottom arm to help you to the surface, turn your head towards your upper shoulder and take in air as your head breaks the water. Once you have breathed, allow your body to go back under the water until you need another breath. The object of this drill is to work out the top part of the kick. When you are usually kicking butterfly, your feet break the surface and therefore encounter little upward resistance. When kicking on your side, you encounter resistance on the upward part of the kick all the time.

You can gain the same benefit by kicking butterfly underwater with both arms extended in front of you as long as your feet do not break the surface.

3. *Kicking with a board*

Just as with all the other strokes, kicking butterfly with a board is a drill, or exercise, I would recommend very strongly. However, it tends to work at the bottom part of the kick more than the top, and therefore I feel that you should use one of the other two drills to supplement kicking with a board.

Land exercises

To help the up part of the kick, lie on your stomach and spread your arms out in front of you on the floor. Gently lift your legs off the ground together. Repeat many times. To make this exercise slightly more difficult, lift your arms up, keeping them straight, at the same time as lifting your legs.

The rest of the land exercises are the same as for freestyle.

Flexibility

Again, most of the flexibility exercises to help you are similar to freestyle. Many top butterfliers have hyperextending legs – legs that bend slightly backwards when straightened (bow out backwards). As this seems to be common amongst many top butterfliers, then we can assume that it is desirable. So, in addition to the suggested flexibility exercises at the end of this book, also touch your toes with crossed legs. Instead of having your feet together and going down to touch your toes, cross your legs

so your feet are close together and your knees are straight. Then go slowly down to touch your toes. Also touch your toes with one knee slightly bent, the other straight. Repeat the other way. However, before doing these exercises, please read the section on flexibility at the end of the book.

Weights

Although I stressed the need for the legs to follow the arms in butterfly, do not forget that I also said, as you improve you can start working on your butterfly kick without it going out of control. Weight-training and circuit training designed to improve your leg muscles will still be beneficial.

63

Starts and Turns

Even if you are just a recreational swimmer, it is likely you will want to look your best while you are swimming. I find it rather strange how some people put so much effort into learning how to swim, and yet do not bother about teaching themselves how to turn. You see somebody swimming good freestyle down the pool, they get to the end, touch the wall, scramble round, then push off to start again. It looks a mess, and what a shame, because it really does not take much time and effort to learn how to turn properly.

The start can be even worse. I am sure you must have watched somebody climb onto the block or onto the side, and get down into a diving position. They hurl their body across the water. They look good. Then they hit the water – flat. You cringe as you hear the sound of the belly-flop. Perhaps starting properly is even more important than turning properly!

If you are a competitive swimmer, then starts and turns are even more important. So often a swimmer will concentrate almost all his time on swimming, and forget that the turn and start are part of the race. When I won my Olympic Gold Medal, I gained quite a considerable distance off all the other finalists on my dive and on my turn, which of course helped me win. All too often, coaches don't feel that it is important enough to spend time in training practising starts and turns, but all it takes is a few minutes a week to see a great improvement. This few minutes a week is well worth it, because to improve your swimming by a comparable amount will take much longer.

Most swimmers see a turn as almost a rest in the middle of their swim. So if you attack the wall and work it hard, you can gain a great advantage. The turn starts at the flags 5 metres from the end of the pool. You set yourself up so you will hit the wall at the right time. It may mean that you will have to adjust your stroke slightly, which is to your advantage. If you have to do this, then you can pick the tempo of your stroke up and therefore gain more off your opposition. Try not to arrive on the wall – hit the wall hard and leave it quickly. Finally, when you push off, check that you are as streamlined as possible. Check your body is in a straight line, that your legs are pushed together and your feet pointed. It is easy to allow your elbows to bend, so be careful. Also remember to try and push your shoulders up towards your ears and squeeze your elbows together. To help me get into this position, I put one hand on top of the other. By doing this I manage to

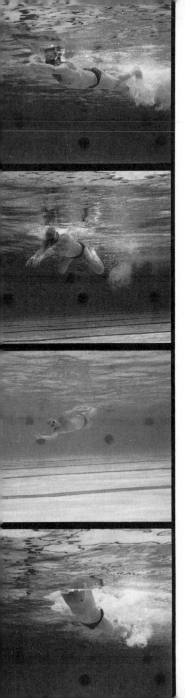

get into an even more streamlined position. As you leave the wall, push off under the water rather than on top of it. By doing this, you are underneath the surface tension which will slow you down. By angling your hands slightly upwards, you can help your legs get your body to the surface. Remember, the further you get on your turn, the less distance you have to swim. Obviously, if you stay underwater too long you will run out of air and tire yourself out.

Judging the wall

For a good turn, it is important to know exactly how far away you are from the wall. You don't want to be caught too close or too far away. If you are too close, it will be hard to turn round. If you are too far away then you have to wait until you reach the wall to turn. If you let either of these things happen, you are giving your competition an edge. So how do you judge how far you are from the wall? Well, there are four methods that you can use:

1. The backstroke flags are 5 metres from the end of the pool, and this is a standard distance.

2. The lane ropes are usually a different colour for the last 5 metres of the pool.

3. The 'T' on the bottom of the pool. Most swimming pools have a black line running on the bottom in each of the

lanes, which stops just before the end of the pool. At the end of the black line there is a little bar that runs across, and hence the name 'T'. There is no standard distance between the end of the 'T' and the wall, so you must be careful using it as a way of judging the distance to the wall. As one end of the pool will be shallow and the other deep, it is easy to misjudge the distance to the wall because at the deep end the 'T' will look closer to the end. This effect is caused by the distance you are from the bottom.

4.   The cross. Most pools, as well as having lines on the bottom, will have a cross on the wall just below the surface of each lane. You may find this cross particularly helpful to your freestyle turn.

Whichever stroke you swim, try and use as many ways as possible to judge the end. Practise turning only and counting how many strokes it is to the wall from the flags. Check that you are swimming into the wall at the same speed as you will be during a race.

One final point before we move onto looking at each of the turns individually; if you are wearing goggles, be careful not to raise your head. Most swimmers are worried about losing their goggles on a turn, and to prevent this they tend to raise their head and look where they are going – that way, the goggles do not come off. However, by

67

doing this, they are breaking the streamlined position and slowing themselves down. So if you feel that you have to wear goggles during a competition, make sure that you practise keeping your head down during training and learn how to keep your goggles on in a streamlined position.

Butterfly and breaststroke turn

I have only depicted one of the two turns. The reason for this is that butterfly and breaststroke turns are very similar. In fact, to all intents and purposes they are the same. Where they differ is that breaststroke has a pull and a kick underwater, and this is why it has been described.

As you come into the wall, try and stop your body dead in the water. Do not let yourself come any closer. This, of course, is obvious when you think about it; after all, you don't want to get any further from the other end. As you touch the end, your hand should be parallel with your shoulders, which in turn are parallel with the water. In some competitions in the United States you are allowed to dip one shoulder down. I turn to my right, however you may feel more comfortable turning to your left.

As I am coming in to touch the wall, I brace my left arm in order to stop my body. The instant my right hand touches the wall, I pull it away. I clench my fist and force my elbow back as hard and

Forcing the elbow back hard and fast

quickly as possible. The more aggress-
ively you pull your elbow back, the
quicker you will turn. This action starts
to twist your body round ready to make
the turn. Meanwhile, I pull my knees up
to my chest. I concentrate on pulling my
left knee up harder and faster than my
right to help the twist that I have started
with my right elbow. Once my right knee
has started to move, I allow my left knee
to drift behind it slightly. As the right
knee is following in the wake of the left,
it is not so difficult to pull the right knee
up. I place my left foot under my left
hand on the wall, and my right foot
slightly to the left of my left hand. By
crossing your legs like this on the wall,
you help your body to twist as you push

off the wall. As your right hand leaves the wall, it is important for it to travel as quickly as possible back into the water. So many breaststrokers and butterfliers keep their arms straight as they recover the top arm, and wave to the crowd (instead of going straight into the water, it goes into an arc over the head and into the water). There are three ways your hand can travel:

1. the hand travels straight past your face, just missing your nose;

2. it goes just over the top of your head, almost touching your head as it passes;

3. it goes just past the back of your head, just missing your ear as it passes your head.

There is no correct way; it is just a question of which one you feel most at ease with. I personally prefer just missing the ear and taking my hand behind my head.

Both your hands now should be travelling as directly as possible towards the other end of the pool. As my left hand is coming over the top of the water, its weight forces my body down under the water level with my feet. As I start to push off from the wall, my body is still at a slight downward angle to the water. As I leave the wall, I straighten up.

Until now, the movements to make a butterfly turn or a breaststroke turn have been the same. However, as you leave the wall a breaststroker can afford to angle his body and push down slightly further than a butterflier. The reason for this is a breaststroker is allowed one pull and one kick underwater before he surfaces.

Once I have left the wall and my body has started to slow in the water, I reach up slightly and start the breaststroke pull. Follow the correct pattern until the point at which you would begin to squeeze your elbows in. Then push down the centre of your body much as you would do in the bottom part of the pull on butterfly. Your hands, in fact, should trace a club-shaped pattern in the water. This movement allows you to take more advantage of the pull, and therefore achieve greater distance.

As your hands touch your thighs, keep them there. It is easy to allow yourself to relax at this point, which means your elbows start to bend. This, of course, causes drag in the water. Concentrate on keeping your feet together and your toes pointed. This will also help you to get more distance out of your underwater pull.

Keeping your hands flat against your body, sneak them up along your body, trying to cause as little resistance as possible. Simultaneously, slowly and gently lift your legs ready to kick. As your hands lunge forward and click into the stretch position, your legs should

71

snap straight. All being well, your head should break the water and you will then be ready to swim breaststroke. However, getting this right isn't particularly easy, so you may have to practise a few times. Obviously in a 200 you can pull a little later and kick a little later and surface a little later – you are not in such a hurry!

As you leave the wall on butterfly, try and get a little depth, especially if you are good at fly kick. (I have seen people capable of swimming dolphin kick underwater almost as quickly as swimming butterfly on the surface.) Do be careful not to use up too much air – this will cause fatigue. Try and find a happy medium that suits you.

It is extremely important to get the distance to the wall right when coming in to turn. It is so easy to catch the turn short or long (taking half a stroke too many or taking half a stroke too few). As you set yourself up for the turn, use the four methods of judging how far you are from the end and try and adjust your stroke so your last one will come over and touch the wall with your arms extended. Breaststrokers, however, will find it more difficult to change their stroke to suit the wall. If you have to, take the wall long rather than short (when in doubt, do not add another stroke). Allow your body to drift underwater and wait until your hands touch the wall before turning.

72

Backstroke turn

The one golden rule is, make sure that you can turn on either side. The reason for this is that you cannot govern which hand is going to touch the wall first. Whenever you swim backstroke, count the strokes in from the flags to the wall so you know exactly where the wall is. Also take note of what angle the flags are when you touch. You want to get this down to such an art that all you have to do is stretch back, and you know your hand will touch the wall with a straight arm. Being able to judge the wall like this will really help your backstroke turn.

As I touch the wall I arch backwards and lift my knees so my feet come out of the water. To help me do this, the hand down to my side is facing the bottom of the pool and pressing down slightly to give me leverage. I then force my feet around, keeping them above the water. This is achieved by pivoting round on my back. However, my main attention is focused on getting my feet from the swimming position to the wall as quickly as possible. By doing this I automatically swivel around on my back. As my feet start to come round, the hand that I touch with starts its journey to join my other hand, ready to push off from the wall. The push off is underwater, as in all the other strokes, using your kick to get yourself to the

73

Backstroke turn – pivot on the back

74

surface. Some people prefer to put a few dolphin leg kicks in while they are underwater – if your butterfly leg kick is better than your backstroke leg kick, you may consider doing this.

I suggest you practise your backstroke turn in the shallow end, away from the wall. Just lie on your back, still in the water, and practise getting your legs up and your feet round. Once you can do this, you will find it easy to do when you have the wall to help you.

Tumble turn

The freestyle tumble turn or, as it is sometimes known, flip turn, has developed because there is no need to touch the end with your hand – your feet, in competition, count as touching the wall. The reason it is called tumble turn is that that is literally what you do – a tumble in the water. As I come into the wall and judge that I am the right distance away to start my turn, I allow my extended arm to slip down in the water towards my opposite knee which will help twist my body over to the side; my shoulder follows my hand by dipping down after it. I then tuck my head in and begin the tumble. My body tries to follow my hand throughout the tumble. As this is happening, I tuck my legs in to assist me. This also makes the turn quicker.

I do not tumble straight over the top,

Push off on your side

but lean to one side. By doing this I land up on my side when my feet are on the wall rather than with my stomach facing the bottom of the pool. Furthermore, I actually push off in this position. There are two reasons for doing this. Firstly, if you go straight over the top in a somersault, you would land up on your back and have to twist your body round before pushing off. This, of course, takes time and is awkward. Secondly, pushing off on your side, you do not drag so much against the bottom (as you swim, you get a certain amount of drag against the bottom, especially in the shallow end).

Do not worry about staying on your side after pushing off the wall. The final part of the tumble turn is probably one of the most abused in swimming. To straighten your body, you must pull your bottom arm (the arm deepest in the water). By doing this, you are not only straightening up your body ready to swim freestyle, but you are also giving

76

yourself a chance for a very good pull. Most swimmers make the mistake of pulling the top arm (the arm closest to the surface). Of course, this does not straighten out the body, and added to this you end up pulling along the surface of the water. Please remember to pull with your bottom arm.

Grab start

Be ready to get on the back of the block; so many swimmers get up and start playing with their goggles, or doing their suit up, etc. I believe all this should be done beforehand. The race has started when you get on the block. You should also watch the races beforehand and take note of how long the starter usually takes to get the competitors on the back of the block and between 'take your marks' and the gun going off.

As you get onto the block and take your marks, make sure your feet are a comfortable distance apart – pretty much the same distance as they would be if you were to jump up in the air.

In my opinion, there are two effective grab starts:

1.   The one pictured on the next page is my favourite. Notice how my thumbs are actually resting on the block, supporting my body weight so I don't topple into the water. Ironically, with this form of grab start you should not actually grab the block (hold the block). Your legs should be bent

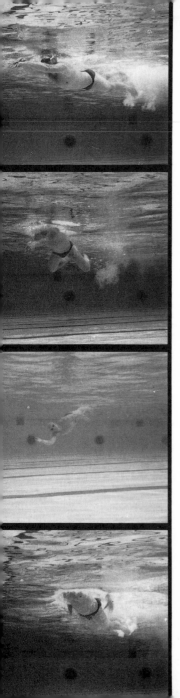

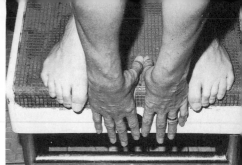

Grab start – feet comfortably apart, thumbs resting on the block

nicely, head up, and you should be looking forward. Lean as far forward as possible.

When the gun goes off, all you have to do is drop your head and your body starts to fall forward. At the same instant, force your hands forward. Try and resist the temptation of pulling down on the block because this action would be a waste of effort – it does not help you to go in the direction in which you want to go.

2. The hands grab the side of the block to prevent your body falling into the water. Lean forward as far as possible. When the gun goes off, all you have to do is let go. The reason I prefer the first grab start is because you can remain slightly more relaxed on the block. But just choose the method that suits you.

Pike dive

It wasn't long ago that swimmers believed they should get into the water as quickly as possible and start swimming. However, by trial and error they found that the pike dive was much faster. The reason for this is that water has a skin on the top that causes friction and slows you down. The idea of a pike dive is to cut through the surface tension as cleanly as possible and travel underwater rather than on top. By doing the pike dive, you not only cut through the surface skin, you also maximize the distance and height of your dive.

I do not only dive outwards, but also upwards as I leave the block. This enables me to get out as far as possible. When I stop travelling forwards and start to fall, I drop my arms and upper body, which forms the pike. As my hands go in the water I arch my back and pull my legs up so they do not touch the water. What you are trying to do is get your body to go through the same hole in the water. The second your hands enter the water, you must angle them towards the end of the pool, but be careful not to do this before you have entered the water. If you do, then you destroy most of the benefit you are trying to gain.

You have now stopped going forward and are falling. As you go down towards the water, the whole angle of your body is pointing more towards the bottom than the end. By arching your back and, once your hands are in the water, angling them towards the end of the pool, you are converting downward 'falling speed' into forward movement.

79

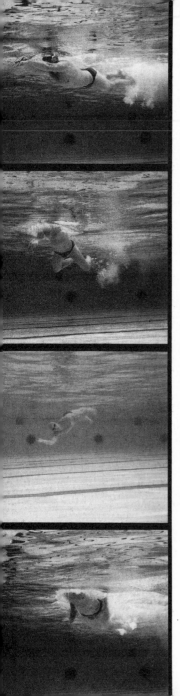

Pike dive

Some swimmers find it fairly easy to pick up the pike dive – I found it extremely tricky. To make it easier, try these five stages. However, beware – practise in the deep end to avoid hitting the bottom.

1.   Sit on the side with your feet in the gutter, and do a little duck dive into the water. Make sure the top of your feet do not hit the surface of the water but follow your legs in.

2.   Crouch on the side, allow yourself to fall forward and extend your legs so you are pushing out over the water. As you get into the water, try to achieve the feeling the duck dive gave you in stage 1.

3.   Stand on the edge, crouch slightly forward and try a slightly more ambitious version of stage 2.

4.   Stand on the block in the same crouched position and try to copy what you have done in stage 3 – which, by now, should hopefully be a pike dive.

5.   Go down into a racing position and simulate what you have done in stage 4.

There is one other method of learning the pike dive, which can also be used to improve it. Get a hula-hoop and place it in the water in the rough vicinity of where you think you will land (get somebody to hold it gently with an outstretched arm). As you dive, try and make your body go through the hula-hoop without hitting it. If you don't do a pike dive, then your legs may well hit the hula-hoop, which can sting a little bit. However, this is an incentive to perform correctly.

Even if you are good at the pike dive, the hula-hoop can help you improve yourself. Put the hula-hoop in a position

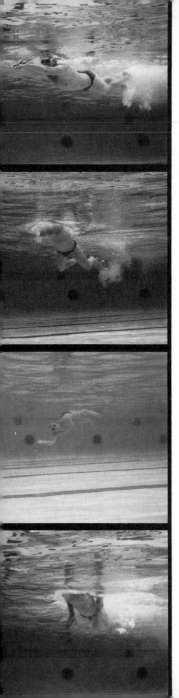

My special breaststroke dive

where you feel comfortable about diving through it. Each time you get through the hoop, get the person holding the hoop to move it a couple of inches further out. See how far you can get the hula-hoop from the side of the pool. This, of course, helps you to find out which angle is best for you.

I developed a rather unorthodox start. Dive out as if you were performing a pike dive, and as you pike your body, pull your feet up towards your backside. This will force you into a more vertical position. Stay in this position until your hands break through the surface of the water, and then kick your legs out as hard as you can, straight up above you. By doing this you are forcing your body down into the water with greater speed. Once in the water, direct your hands towards the end of the pool and arch your back. Because you are forcing yourself slightly deeper into the water, this dive will not be suitable for any stroke other than breaststroke.

82

Flexibility and Swimming

Generally speaking, the looser your joints and muscles are, the easier it is to move and consequently swim. Another reason for working on flexibility is, the more supple you are, the less likely you are to get injured.

The stretching exercises on the following pages are the minimum I would recommend for a serious swimmer, and I think they speak for themselves. Do not overstretch. Stop at the point where you feel your muscles pulling so tightly they start to hurt. If you overstretch, you will pull your muscles and cause scar tissue to form, which will cause tightening.

To prevent this happening, make sure you are warmed up before you start your flexibility exercises. This can be done by jogging a few times around the pool, but be sure to wear running shoes so as not to damage your shin muscles. Once your legs are warmed up, gently start circling your arms forwards, backwards and in opposite directions, one at a time and together. Make sure you reach as high as possible and as low as possible as you swing them, and touch your ear to your arm as they pass. This should help the top half of your body warm up.

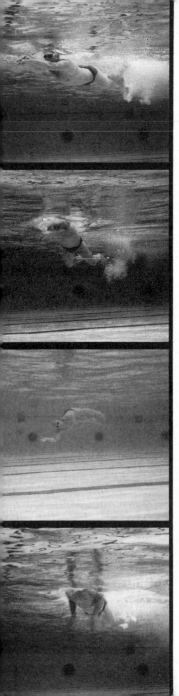

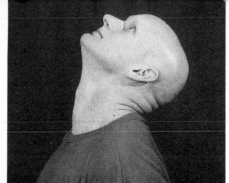

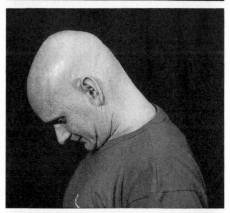

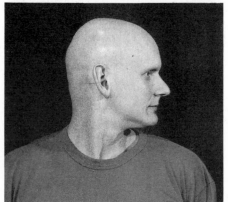

Neck stretching

84

Stretch as high as you can and press your hands back

Push forward

Push back and up

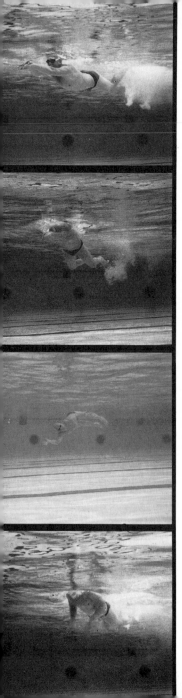

Head towards knees

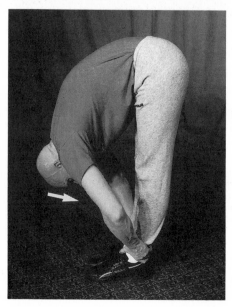

Don't forget to repeat on other leg

87

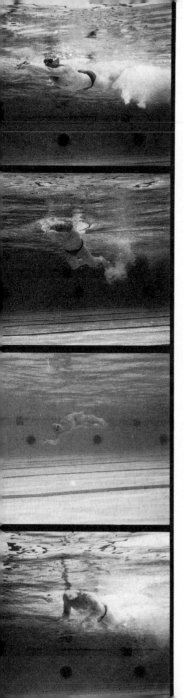

Push knee towards floor

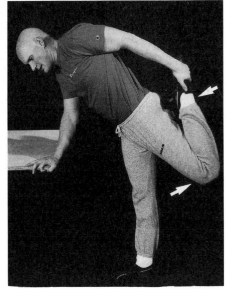

Pull foot towards backside and push knee back

89

Sequence E:
Freestyle catch-up
drill

Sequence F:
Breaststroke
submarine drill

Push knees outwards and downwards with elbows

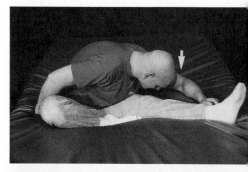

Sequence G:
Butterfly kick
on side drill

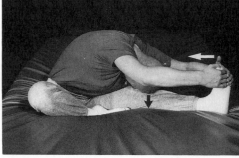

Sequence H:
Butterfly one and
double armed drill

Head to knee and gently pull foot towards you

90

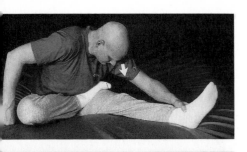

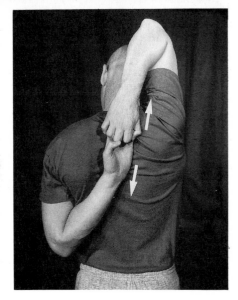

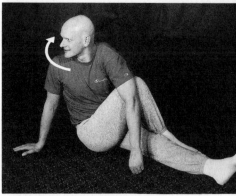

When you go into the stretch position, do so gently. Do not jerk or bounce the muscle, as this will also cause scar tissue to form. When you feel that you are stretching the muscle, stop and remain in that position for at least six seconds. If you feel it stretch too much, relax slightly. After each exercise, shake out the muscle.

You will notice that in the illustrations I am wearing a tracksuit. This is to keep my muscles warm while stretching.

It's worth emphasizing again, if you feel any pain, *stop immediately*.

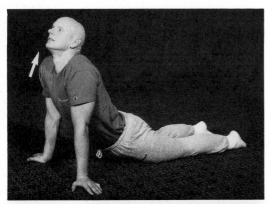

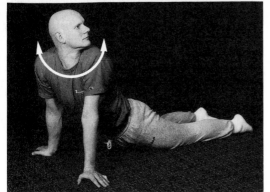

Land Training

There are two aspects to land training:

1. Working on increasing heart and lung capacities and muscle endurance.
2. Increasing strength through weight-training.

Throughout the book I have suggested out-of-the-water exercises which will help toughen certain groups of muscles for a particular stroke. However, if you want to be a competitive swimmer then I suggest you read the following section.

Although swimming is the best all round exercise, to get to the top of competitive swimming you must look for ways of getting the edge over your rivals. Therefore, most serious swimmers spend a considerable amount of time land training.

I believe to achieve a good land programme you should try and balance the body. For example, as I have mentioned earlier, swimming tends to build up the triceps (the back of the upper arm); to counteract this, your land training should not only include your triceps but especially your biceps (the front of the upper arm). The benefits will not only be a better general strength, but also you will be less likely to tie-up*.

Most swimmers tend to run quite a bit at the beginning of the season to strengthen their leg muscles. It also helps them get their heart and lungs into good shape before starting 'two-a-days' (two swimming workouts in one day). Running can be substituted for any other sport that works the leg and lungs, e.g. cycling, basketball, squash etc.

Circuit training

Remember to warm up and stretch first.

You can develop a circuit with or without weights. A good circuit should workout all the muscle groups throughout the

* Tie-up is a swimming term for muscles tightening up at the end of a race.